If it can't be fun, it can't be done
... even without the gluten

FREE IN THE KITCHEN

A GLUTEN-FREE COOKBOOK

By Sallie Powell

Disclaimer: The consulting services of Gluten Freedom are strictly related to reducing the stress of starting a gluten-free diet. This program does not offer nutritional or medical advice or information. If you suspect that gluten may be a problem for you, you should consult with your doctor before eliminating gluten from your diet.

ISBN 978-0-692-56508-7

Printed in the United States of America

First Edition

Editor: Susan Trainor // *Interior design layout:* Lori Danello Roberts // *Cover and publicity photos:* Sally Sox // *Additional photos:* Sallie Powell

For Bob, the love of my life.

You have enjoyed and endured
my culinary triumphs and failures since 1978.

You are my greatest encourager.

With you by my side, life is always fun.

welcome to ...
FREE IN THE KITCHEN

WCTV: Good Morning Show

Author Sallie Powell with co-hosts Shonda Knight and Art Myers on The Good Morning Show, WCTV

If I had to choose one word to describe the reason why I wrote this book, it would be encouragement. There really is life after gluten, especially when your whole food world seems to be turned upside down by taking it out of your diet. After barely eating anything for a year, I felt trapped by my decision not to eat gluten. Today, I am free. The negative has been turned into a positive, and now my kitchen is full of wonderful food options. I no longer live without, but live fully and freely. It is my hope that you, too, will find newfound freedom as you move into your gluten-free lifestyle.

For years my life's motto has been "If it can't be fun, it can't be done." This positive attitude has seen me through many ups and downs and has been the banner over my new food adventure. Part of my fun is creating new gluten-free recipes. Another part is being able to share these recipes on our local television station, WCTV. Since the end of 2012, I have been filming gluten-free food segments as a community service for our audiences.

How it all began

"Mom, I just don't feel well."

I heard this over and over again, from the time my youngest daughter, Bethany, was old enough to express herself to the historic day she was diagnosed with celiac disease. Before her diagnosis, the medical community could give us no solid answers. Throughout my daughter's childhood, the mystery of her frequent bouts with illness was always excused away to the ordinary ... a bad virus ... indoor allergies ... outdoor allergies ... the weather.

Author Sallie Powell and daughter Bethany

Adding to her misery was my hobby. I am a baker and a serious one at that. I used to grind my own wheat berries and even put in extra gluten to improve my bread's texture. I kept feeding this dear child nutritious, homemade bread, expecting it to heal all her ailments. Don't feel well? Here, have another slice.

When Bethany got older, she started putting together the pieces of her health puzzle. Through hours, days, weeks, and years of reading and research borne out of her desperation to be well, she became her own trained health detective. I'll never forget *the* phone call. I was skeptical at first. Dead ends tend to make you that way.

Thankfully, at age 27, Bethany's determination to follow up on what she had learned on her own sent her to seek medical confirmation from her doctor. When she presented her newfound information to her physician, he concurred and ordered the necessary testing. First a blood test. *Positive.* Then an endoscopy with a biopsy of the small intestine. *Positive.*

Now what? I believe the proverb "Necessity is the mother of invention" applies here. And we needed to eat. Since I shared many of the same symptoms with my daughter, I decided to follow my doctor's suggestion: "If you feel better without gluten, don't eat it." As a result of feeling so much better without gluten, along with my daughter's new diagnosis, I found a new passion: inventing and reinventing the tastiest and most nutritious gluten-free dishes for my family and friends.

The comical element of this food adventure is that I don't particularly like to cook. This also may be true for many of you. As a child, my cue to run outside and play was when my mother stepped into the kitchen to cook. I ran away from cooking when many of my friends were enjoying learning how to bake a cake or put together a casserole. So, to make being in the kitchen doable for me, I spell cook: *c-r-e-a-t-e.* This has always been true of my baking hobby and is now true of my new passion for creating gluten-free dishes.

Cooking is work. Creating is fun.

About Sallie ...

SALLIE DIDN'T START cooking until she absolutely had to. With a hungry husband and three young mouths to feed, she felt "doomed" to spend hours in the kitchen—until she added two ingredients to all her recipes: fun and creativity. Years later, these two ingredients would be essential to living a gluten-free lifestyle.

With her daughter's diagnosis of celiac disease and her own intolerance of gluten, Sallie was overwhelmed by a kitchen full of food labels. But with determination and hope for a new beginning, the chains of the unknown dropped away. Writing new gluten-free recipes and rewriting family favorites became simple and fun. Sallie was "free in the kitchen" once again!

An encourager at heart, Sallie loves to free others by helping to coordinate gluten-free menus for individuals and events. As a community service since 2012, she also enjoys sharing her recipes on Tallahassee's local CBS affiliate, WCTV. Her food journey has been deeply enriched by her husband, Bob, her amazing daughters and sons-in-law, and six very near perfect grandchildren.

What I Think About Gluten

IS IT JUST A FAD? I sure do wish so. And honestly, for some it may be. But for those who have been diagnosed with celiac disease and for those who cannot tolerate gluten, it is far from a fad.

The obvious truth is that our systems are sensitive, some more than others, and it's just smart to pay attention to what we eat. Whether it is gluten, dairy, soy, or anything else you suspect is an issue, respecting what your body can tolerate is of utmost importance. With that in mind and with the assistance of trained professionals, improved health might be just a bite away. Much research has already been done, and fortunately for us, there is still much more being done. With all the different views, relying on facts and the advice of trusted physicians is a better safety net than trying to decide which food fad to follow.

Here is my honest confession. In the not so distant past, I never really listened to my body. In fact, I would never let it speak. I'd rather have the cream-filled doughnut and hurt later. The satisfaction of that creamy delicacy was far greater than any discipline I could muster. If the truth was further told, caring for what my body actually needed was of little importance to me.

Then came the pizza dilemma. My desire to have a slice eventually was replaced with being sorry I had taken the first bite. The grim reality was that the medicines to survive eating the pizza cost me more than the pizza itself. That's when I started listening to what my body was saying. Learning to listen to my body was one of the smartest things I ever did. Learning to give my body a voice was even smarter. Undisciplined food cravings can silence the voice.

CONTENTS

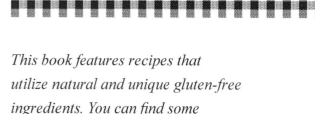

This book features recipes that utilize natural and unique gluten-free ingredients. You can find some of my personal favorites in the **GLUTEN-FREE PANTRY STAPLES** *on pages 76 and 77.*

chapter 1
LITTLE BITES

In the beginning, gluten-free living may be a challenge.
But a challenge is not a wall; a challenge is a door to open,
with many good possibilities waiting for you on the other side.

Brie Bites

Bold, nutty, and sweet—Brie Bites are the perfect food guest at any party.

FROM THE PANTRY

19.6-ounce wheel Brie cheese

1/2 cup chopped walnuts

1/2 cup chopped dried cranberries

1/2 cup brown sugar

16 ounces gluten-free pie crust mix

HOW TO CREATE

Preheat oven to 350°.

Combine walnuts, cranberries, and brown sugar. Set aside.

Using very small scoop (measuring about 1 teaspoon), scoop dough into lightly oiled mini muffin tin. Press into bottom and up sides, keeping dough floured to prevent sticking.

Spoon 1/2 teaspoon of walnut mixture into each muffin cup.

Trim rind from Brie, cut into 3/4-inch pieces, and place on top of walnut mixture.

For third layer, carefully spoon 1/2 teaspoon of walnut mixture on top of Brie.
Bake for 20-25 minutes.

Cool in muffin tin for 5 minutes, and then remove Brie Bites to cooling rack.

This wooden dowel is the perfect tool for pressing dough into a mini muffin cup to form a crust.

Yields 48 appetizers; recipe easily halved to yield 24

Crab Stuffed Mushrooms

FROM THE PANTRY

24 ounces white mushrooms, 12-14

1 cup fresh lump crabmeat

1/2 cup cream cheese, softened at room temperature

1/2 cup chopped fresh parsley

1/2 cup chopped green onions

5 tablespoons fresh Parmesan cheese, divided

1/4 teaspoon salt

1 teaspoon garlic powder

2 slices gluten-free bread

HOW TO CREATE

Preheat oven to 350°.

Brush mushrooms with a soft, moist cloth and gently remove stems. Combine crabmeat, cream cheese, parsley, onions, 4 tablespoons Parmesan cheese, salt, and garlic powder.

In food processor, pulse 2 gluten-free bread slices into small crumbs. Mix crumbs with 1 tablespoon Parmesan cheese. Put 1 tablespoon crabmeat mixture in each mushroom. Cover top of each mushroom with bread crumbs. Bake for 20 minutes or until golden brown.

Yields 12-14 appetizers

Whether on the football field or in the kitchen, my grandson, Brice Williamson, makes the plays that bring on cheers! These stuffed mushrooms were no challenge to this self-made chef.

Even in a recipe as simple this, three ingredients can be overwhelming to someone new to a gluten-free diet.

Sausage Dip

Sometimes you need simple and easy with a huge taste. This sausage dip is tried and true, and with the right brands can still be part of a gluten-free menu. Add another 8 ounces of cream cheese for a creamier consistency, and serve warm in a crock pot with various veggies and gluten-free chips and crackers.

FROM THE PANTRY

2 pounds ground sausage

8 ounces cream cheese

2 10-ounce cans Ro∗Tel tomatoes, original, mild, or hot

HOW TO CREATE

Brown and drain sausage.

Drain Ro∗Tel and add to sausage. Add cream cheese. Mix well.

Yields 32 two-tablespoon servings

Ham and Cucumber Pinwheels

"It's a wrap!" is easy to say when assembling these colorful pinwheels. Their performance at any event will be highly applauded and remembered as real crowd pleasers! Just remember to tuck and roll!

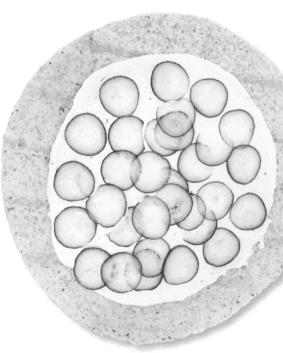

FROM THE PANTRY

6 wraps, original, garden vegetable, spinach, or tomato

1/2 pound honey ham, very thinly sliced

4 baby cucumbers, thinly sliced

2 cups plain Greek yogurt

1-ounce packet gluten-free dry ranch dressing mix

HOW TO CREATE

To make the dressing, mix yogurt and dressing mix, and chill for at least an hour.

Wash and slice cucumbers very thin. Spread 2 tablespoons dressing on wrap, spreading to within 1 inch of edge.

Place cucumbers randomly on top of dressing.
Place 2 slices of ham on top of cucumbers.

Tuck ingredients as you tightly roll wrap from one side to the other, forming a "log." Trim excess wrap off two ends, cut in half, and then cut each half into 3 pieces, making 6 pinwheels per wrap.

Place on serving dish and cover with plastic wrap until ready to serve. Put unused dressing on the side for serving.

Yields 36 appetizers

Italian Cream Cheese Pinwheels

Leaving the ranch and putting a little bit of Italy in these pinwheels shows the versatility of the multi-useful wrap. Make your own version with your favorite veggies and meats, remembering to keep your slices very thin so ... You'll be ready to roll!

HOW TO CREATE

Combine cream cheese and dressing mix, and mix well (at least 1 minute). Let sit for at least an hour.

Chop drained tomatoes.

Spread 2 tablespoons cream cheese mixture on wrap, spreading to within 1 inch of edge. Place single layer of spinach leaves on top of cream cheese. Place 2-1/2 tablespoons tomatoes on top of spinach.

Tuck ingredients as you tightly roll from one side to the other, forming a "log." Trim excess wrap off two ends, cut in half, and then cut each half into 3 pieces, making 6 pinwheels per wrap.

Yields 36 appetizers

FROM THE PANTRY

6 wraps, original, garden vegetable, spinach, or tomato

8 ounces cream cheese, softened at room temperature

.70-ounce packet gluten-free dry Italian dressing mix

2 cups baby spinach leaves

1 cup oven-dried Roma red tomatoes, drained

Penne and Roasted Vegetable Salad

Summertime gardens are usually filled with squash, peppers, tomatoes, and onions.
Here is a perfect way to combine them all into one big summertime memory.

FROM THE PANTRY

8 ounces quinoa penne pasta

4 cups chicken broth

4 yellow squash

4 zucchini

1 red pepper

1 yellow or orange pepper

1 small sweet onion

1-1/2 cups cherry tomatoes, halved

4 garlic cloves, sliced

2 tablespoons fresh basil

2 tablespoons olive oil

1 tablespoon Italian seasoning

1 teaspoon salt

1 pound Boar's Head sandwich pepperoni

2-3 tablespoons capers

DRESSING

1/2 cup olive oil

1 tablespoon white wine herb vinegar

1 garlic clove, chopped

1 teaspoon Italian seasoning

1 teaspoon sugar

HOW TO CREATE

Bring chicken broth to boil, add pasta, and simmer until noodles are tender. The broth will continue to be absorbed while pasta is cooling.

Preheat oven to 425°. Cut yellow squash and zucchini in half and in half again. Cut each strip into 1-inch pieces. Slice peppers and onion into thin strips. Cut cherry tomatoes into halves. Add garlic and basil. Toss all vegetables in large bowl with olive oil, Italian seasoning, and salt. Place on large foil-lined baking sheet, making sure vegetables are spread in thin layer. Roast for 25-30 minutes, stirring once.

Cut sandwich pepperoni into small pieces. In large bowl, toss pepperoni, pasta, roasted vegetables, and capers.

To make dressing, combine olive oil, vinegar, garlic, Italian seasoning, and sugar. Toss with pasta and vegetables.

Serves 6-8

I'm homemade— just like all my recipes— a mixture of trial and error, success and failure.

Lime or lemon zest is quick and easy with this handy tool.

Summer Salad Medley

Summer gardens yield many of the veggies in this salad. Combined with a rice medley, this is a great side dish or a complete meal when you add chopped chicken or shrimp.

DRESSING

3/4 cup light olive oil

1/2 cup citrus
Champagne vinegar

1 teaspoon lemon zest

2 tablespoons sugar

1/2 teaspoon salt

FROM THE PANTRY

1 cup basmati rice medley

2 cups chicken broth

1 cup carrots

3/4 cup Vidalia onion

3/4 cup celery

1 red bell pepper

3 garlic cloves

1/2 cup fresh parsley

1 cup mushrooms

1 cup mini cucumbers

1/2 cup scallions

HOW TO CREATE

Cook rice with chicken broth according to directions on package. Set aside to cool.

Dice and microwave carrots for 3 minutes in just enough water to cover them. Drain and cool.

Chop onion, celery, red pepper, garlic, parsley, mushrooms, cucumber, and scallions. Toss with rice and carrots.

To make dressing, combine olive oil, vinegar, lemon zest, sugar, and salt. Pour desired amount of dressing over rice salad and mix well. Add salt and lemon juice to taste.

Serves 4

FROM THE PANTRY

1/4 cup olive oil

12 ounces orzo, 1-1/2 cups

3 garlic cloves, chopped

1/2 cup pine nuts

1/4 teaspoon salt

2 teaspoons basil

2 teaspoons oregano

2 teaspoons thyme

2-3/4 cups chicken broth

2 cups finely chopped
fresh spinach

1/4 cup black or
Kalamata olives

1/2 cup chopped sun-dried
tomatoes

1/2 cup chopped red pepper

1/2 cup feta cheese

1/4 cup Ken's Italian Dressing

Orzo Spinach Salad

The rice-shaped pasta, orzo, was the inspiration for this flavorful salad. Like links of a chain, each ingredient follows the other in a natural progression of complementary tastes.

HOW TO CREATE

Warm olive oil in large skillet on medium heat. Add orzo, garlic, pine nuts, and salt. Sauté until light golden brown. Add basil, oregano, thyme, and chicken broth. Bring to boil, reduce heat to simmer, and then cover. Simmer until broth is absorbed, approximately 20-25 minutes. Stir twice to prevent sticking. Set aside to cool.

In large bowl, toss spinach, olives, tomatoes, and pepper.
Add rice and toss gently with cheese and dressing.

To make it a meal, add chicken, beef, or shrimp.

Serves 4-6

Christmas in July Salad

How do you begin a series of summer salad segments for TV when the first one is in July? Why, make it about Christmas, of course. Starting with tiny Christmas trees—broccoli—decorate your trees with the vibrant colors of Christmas. This is a great summer cooking activity for children!

FROM THE PANTRY

1 large bunch broccoli

1 red pepper

1 orange pepper

1 yellow pepper

2 cups cherry or variety blend tomatoes

1 cup finely chopped sweet onion

1 cup sweet baby gold and white corn

1 cup chopped walnuts

1 cup Kerrygold Dubliner cheese

DRESSING

1 cup mayonnaise

5.3-ounce cup plain Greek yogurt

1 tablespoon white wine vinegar

1 tablespoon sugar

HOW TO CREATE

Wash and cut broccoli into very small "trees." Steam broccoli in covered microwave dish with 1/4 cup water for 3 minutes. Immediately drain, rinse with cool water, and continue to cool in bowl of ice and cold water. Set aside to drain in colander.

Wash and remove stems, seeds, and membranes from all peppers. Chop into very small pieces. Slice larger tomatoes in half. Toss broccoli, peppers, tomatoes, and onion in large bowl.

Steam corn in covered microwave dish for 3-4 minutes. Drain and set aside to cool.

Chop cheese into tiny cubes, and add to vegetables along with walnuts and cooled corn.

To make dressing, thoroughly combine mayonnaise, yogurt, vinegar, and sugar. You may adjust vinegar and sugar to taste. Toss with salad or serve on the side.

Serves 6-8

Seven Layer Salad

This recipe started with my mom and was passed along to my sister and me. Bringing this old family favorite into the 21st century was easy by substituting a spinach and kale blend for iceberg lettuce and a Greek yogurt blend for mayonnaise.

FROM THE PANTRY

1 pound baby spinach/baby kale blend

2 red peppers, chopped

1 small onion, chopped

8 ounces shredded cheddar cheese

15 ounces frozen English peas

1 pound bacon

2 cups plain Greek yogurt

1/2 cup sour cream

1-ounce packet gluten-free dry ranch dressing mix

HOW TO CREATE

Tear spinach and kale into small pieces, and place in bottom of trifle bowl.

Continue making layers with next 4 ingredients.

Cook bacon until crispy. Drain thoroughly and chop into very small pieces. Reserve 1/4 cup and layer rest of bacon on top of peas.

Mix yogurt, sour cream, and dressing mix, and spread evenly on top of layered ingredients. Sprinkle with reserved bacon pieces.

Cover and refrigerate overnight.

Serves 10

Taco Salad
WITH AVOCADO DRESSING

Since green is my favorite color, you'd think I would have known about the avocado long before I did. Now that I do, this favorite fruit is a taste I often crave and one that adds the crowning touch to this taco salad. Wanting to perfect the dressing, and knowing I had less than 24 hours before a TV segment, I tried and failed and panicked four times before finally coming up with a simple blend of seven ingredients.

FROM THE PANTRY

1 pound ground beef or turkey

1 packet gluten-free taco seasoning

3/4 cup water

4 gluten-free wraps

1 teaspoon garlic salt

1 tablespoon olive oil

2 cups diced fresh tomatoes

4 cups shredded lettuce, any kind

1 cup sweet onion, diced

3.8-ounce can sliced black olives

1 cup chopped cilantro

15.5-ounce can pink beans, drained

15.5-ounce can black beans, drained

2 cups shredded cheese, cheddar or Mexican blend

DRESSING

2 avocados

5.3-ounce cup plain Greek yogurt

Juice from 1/2 lime

1 teaspoon dry cilantro

1 teaspoon sugar

2 tablespoons olive oil

1 teaspoon garlic salt

HOW TO CREATE

Brown and drain meat, and then add seasoning and water. Simmer until water is absorbed.

Preheat oven to 350°. Brush wraps with olive oil. Sprinkle lightly with garlic salt. Place each wrap in taco bowl pan, pressing wrap inside bowl with oiled side up. Bake for 5-7 minutes, watching shells carefully so they don't over bake. Cool in pans.

To make dressing, remove meat from avocados and place in medium bowl. Add yogurt, lime juice, cilantro, sugar, olive oil, and garlic salt. Stir to combine.

Place lettuce in taco bowl, and then begin layering with onion, olives, cilantro, beans, meat, and cheese. Top with avocado dressing.

Serves 4

Watermelon Salad

I was shocked by the first watermelon salad I saw. "Why would anyone want to ruin a perfectly good watermelon by adding something to it?" I knew why after my first bite! Although I still love to eat the juicy half-circle slices like my grandson Bear Williamson does, I often crave the luscious blend of sweet and savory in this chilled, refreshing salad introduced to me by a good friend.

HOW TO CHIFFONADE

Stack, roll, and slice.

Stack basil leaves and roll them lengthwise into a tight cigar shape. Using your sharpest knife, slice across the roll. Fluff the chiffonade with your fingertips to separate the ribbons. Cut edges will darken quickly, so add the chiffonade to your other ingredient(s) immediately.

FROM THE PANTRY

Seedless watermelon, cubed (about 8 cups)

1-ounce package fresh basil

8 ounces feta cheese, crumbled

1 cup chopped purple onion

1/2 cup balsamic vinegar

1/8 cup sugar

1/4 teaspoon salt

1/2 cup extra virgin olive oil

Serves 8

HOW TO CREATE

Cut watermelon into 1-inch cubes and place in large mixing bowl.

Using chiffonade chopping technique, cut basil into little ribbons. Add to watermelon.

Add feta and onion, and toss with watermelon. Chill in refrigerator.

In small bowl or dressing shaker, combine vinegar, sugar, salt, and olive oil until well blended. Before serving salad, add dressing and toss well.

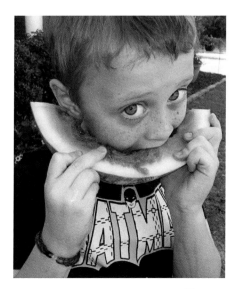

Buffalo Chicken Salad

This sauce combination is known throughout our family as "Bob's Creation." He gets total credit for the perfect blend of sweet with heat. This bursting barbeque flavor is the perfect finishing touch to ribs and wings, too.

FROM THE PANTRY

2 large chicken breasts

1/2 teaspoon salt

1 egg, beaten

3/4 cup gluten-free all-purpose flour

1/2 teaspoon garlic salt

1/4 cup oil

1 head green leaf lettuce

3 salad cucumbers

1 cup shredded carrots

4 ounces crumbled blue cheese or shredded cheddar cheese

1 cup Sweet Baby Ray's Barbeque Sauce

1/4 cup Ken's Honey Mustard Dressing

1/8 teaspoon Frank's Buffalo Wing Sauce

Ken's Blue Cheese or Ranch Dressing

HOW TO CREATE

Combine flour and garlic salt. Sprinkle salt on chicken, and then cut into bite-sized pieces. Dip chicken in egg. Coat each piece of chicken with flour mixture. Heat oil on medium-high heat and fry each chicken piece until golden brown and juices are clear. Drain on paper towel.

Prepare lettuce by washing and cutting into bite-sized pieces. Divide into four large salad bowls. Slice cucumbers into small pieces and place on top of lettuce. Top with carrots and choice of cheese.

In medium bowl, mix barbeque sauce, honey mustard, and wing sauce. Dip fried chicken into sauce mixture and shake off excess. Place chicken pieces on top of salads and serve with blue cheese or ranch dressing.

Serves 4

Chicken Noodle Salad

MARINADE & DRESSING

1 cup light olive oil

4 tablespoons lemon juice

2 teaspoons deli mustard

4 garlic cloves, chopped

1 teaspoon sugar

1 teaspoon basil

1 teaspoon oregano

1/2 teaspoon thyme

1/2 teaspoon garlic salt

1/4 teaspoon pepper

1/4 teaspoon salt

Waiting for a huge pot of water to boil is boring. So, take the boring out of the boil and simmer your favorite pasta in chicken broth for a rich taste and a firm texture. The difference will put a smile on your face and nutrition on your plate.

FROM THE PANTRY

2-3 chicken breasts

5 snack-size cucumbers, cut into small cubes

1 large pepper, red, yellow, or orange, chopped

2 cups cherry tomatoes

4 cups kale and spinach blend

8 ounces Tresomega brand quinoa spaghetti pasta

4 cups chicken broth

Serves 4

HOW TO CREATE

Combine marinade/dressing ingredients. Set aside.

Prepare chicken by cutting into 1-inch pieces. Combine chicken pieces with 1/3 cup marinade/dressing. Set aside to marinate for at least 1 hour or overnight.

Bring broth to boil, break noodles into 2-inch pieces, and simmer on low until noodles are tender. Broth will continue to be absorbed while noodles cool.

Preheat oven to 400°. Bake chicken for 10 minutes, stir and turn chicken pieces, and then bake another 5 minutes. Set aside to cool.

Place cucumbers, pepper, tomatoes, cooled chicken, and noodles in large bowl. Toss with desired amount of remaining marinade/dressing. Serve over kale and spinach blend.

Chicken with Potato Cream Sauce

A mouthful of warmth and comfort awaits you as you take in the flavorful combination of a baked potato and chicken pie.

FROM THE PANTRY

2 cups chopped cooked chicken

2-1/2 cups chicken broth

4 tablespoons potato flour

1/2 teaspoon salt

1/8 teaspoon pepper

1/2 cup sour cream

3 tablespoons chopped fresh chives

4 slices bacon

1 cup frozen petite peas

1 cup diced carrots

Gluten-free pie dough, ready made

Yes, potatoes are a starch, and they are gluten free!

HOW TO CREATE

Preheat oven to 375°.

Place chicken pieces in large mixing bowl.

Cover peas and carrots with water and cook for 10-12 minutes. Drain well and combine with chicken.

Cook bacon until crispy, drain, and chop into tiny pieces. Set aside.

In medium saucepan, briskly whisk potato flour with broth, add salt and pepper, and bring to simmer. Stir until thickened. Potato flour lumps easily, so you may want to use a blender to make your sauce smooth.

Remove potato flour broth from burner, add sour cream, chives, and bacon, and mix well. Pour potato cream sauce over meat and vegetables, and then stir to combine. Place in pie plate or individual baking dishes. Cover mixture with your favorite gluten-free pie crust and bake for 20 minutes.

Serves 6

Stuffed Acorn Squash

Stuffed in an acorn squash bowl, this well-balanced meal is sure to satisfy your cravings for an easy prep and a hearty dish.

FROM THE PANTRY

2 acorn squash

1/2 cup chopped onion

1/2 cup chopped celery

2 tablespoons butter

1 cup crumbled sage-flavored sausage

1 cup gluten-free stuffing

1/4 cup corn flour

1/2 teaspoon salt

1 teaspoon parsley

3/4 cup chicken broth

1 egg, slightly beaten

HOW TO CREATE

Preheat oven to 350°.

Cut squash in half from stem to bottom and scoop out seeds to form squash bowls. Lightly salt inside of each bowl.

Sauté onion and celery in butter for 2-3 minutes. Set aside.

Cook and drain sausage.

In large bowl, combine stuffing, corn flour, salt, and parsley. Add onion, celery, sausage, chicken broth, and egg, and mix thoroughly. If mixture is a little dry, add 2-3 more tablespoons of broth. Spoon 1/4 of mixture into each squash bowl.

Loosely cover each squash bowl with foil and place in small pan with 1/2 cup water. Bake for 1 hour. Remove foil and bake for additional 15 minutes.

Serves 4

Shepherd's Pie
WITH GARLIC SMASHED POTATOES

Shepherd's Pie has been around since the 1700's and with each century has taken on new and different flavors. Topping this timeless recipe with garlic smashed potatoes gives it a modern taste from our century. Bob, this one's for you!

FROM THE PANTRY

3 pounds small red potatoes

6-8 garlic cloves, chopped

2 teaspoons salt, divided

4 cups chicken broth

1 cup sour cream

18 ounces frozen English peas

3 cups carrots, cut into 1-inch pieces

1-1/2 pounds ground beef or turkey

1 teaspoon garlic powder

1 teaspoon onion powder

1 packet McCormick Gluten-Free Brown Gravy

1 cup hot water

HOW TO CREATE

Wash and quarter unpeeled potatoes. Place in Dutch oven with 1 teaspoon salt, garlic, and cover with chicken broth. Bring to boil, lower to medium heat, and cook until tender, stirring occasionally.

Cook carrots on low boil for 5 minutes. Add peas and bring to low boil again, cooking for another 5 minutes. Drain vegetables and place in bottom of 8x12 casserole dish.

Preheat oven to 350°.

Brown ground meat, adding 1 teaspoon salt, garlic powder, and onion powder. Drain well and layer on top of peas and carrots.

Combine hot water with brown gravy mix. Whisk until smooth and pour over meat and vegetables.

When potatoes and garlic are tender, mash them well. (Do not drain potatoes; broth will be absorbed.) Add sour cream and mix thoroughly. Layer potato mixture on top of meat. Bake uncovered for 30 minutes. Cool for 5 minutes, and then serve.

Serves 8-10

Mexican Meatballs
WITH BLACK BEANS AND RICE

Inspired by Bethany, these meatballs went Mexican with south of the border spices, black beans, and salsa! Top with black olives, sour cream, and extra cheese for added flavors.

FROM THE PANTRY

1 cup chunky salsa

3 cups chicken broth

15-ounce can black beans, drained and rinsed

3/4 cup brown rice

2 pounds ground turkey

2 eggs

1/4 cup milk

1 teaspoon salt

1/2 teaspoon onion powder

1 teaspoon dry cilantro

1/2 teaspoon cumin

1 teaspoon garlic powder

1/2 cup finely shredded Mexican blend cheese

HOW TO CREATE

In medium saucepan, combine and stir salsa and broth. Bring to boil. Add rice and black beans. Bring to boil again, cover, and simmer on low for 45 minutes. Stir, re-cover, and then continue simmering another 10-15 minutes. Remove lid, remove from burner, and stir.

Preheat oven to 375°.

In large mixing bowl, combine ground turkey, eggs, milk, seasonings, and cheese. Mix well.

With rounded scoop, place 2 heaping tablespoons of meat mixture into each cup of 24-cup mini muffin tin. Place muffin tin on cookie sheet with sides to catch juices. Bake for 25 minutes. Remove meatballs to wire rack to drain and cool slightly.

Serve meatballs on top or to side of beans and rice. Top with desired toppings.

Serves 4-6

Rice With Kielbasa

Home cooked, one pot, few ingredients. Simple. Quick. Tasteful.

FROM THE PANTRY

6-ounce package Spanish rice mix with seasoning packet

14.5-ounce can diced tomatoes

2 garlic cloves, chopped

1 medium onion, chopped

2 cups frozen English peas

13 ounces turkey kielbasa, cut into bite-sized pieces

1 tablespoon olive oil

2-1/4 cups chicken broth

HOW TO CREATE

In large pan, sauté garlic and onion in olive oil for 3 minutes. Add kielbasa and sauté for additional minute.

Add tomatoes, chicken broth, rice, seasoning packet, and peas to vegetable and meat mixture.

Bring to slight boil, cover, simmer on low heat for approximately 35 minutes, and then let stand for about 5 minutes before serving (keep covered). Liquid will be absorbed while dish stands.

Serves 4-6

Cornbread Taco Pie

This creamy cornbread loaded with taco seasoned meat with a hint of green chilies is sure to send your taste buds south of the border. After making my own seasoning for far too long, I almost kissed the first packet of gluten-free taco seasoning I found in a store!

FROM THE PANTRY

1 pound ground beef

1.25-ounce packet gluten-free taco seasoning

3/4 cup water

1-3/4 cups corn flour

2 teaspoons baking powder

1 teaspoon salt

1 teaspoon xanthan gum

2 teaspoons sugar

2 cups shredded cheddar or Mexican blend cheese, divided

4-ounce can diced green chilies, mild or hot

2 eggs

1 cup milk

1/2 cup sour cream

4 tablespoons melted butter

HOW TO CREATE

Preheat oven to 400°.

Brown ground beef, drain, and put back into pan. Stir in taco seasoning and water. Bring to boil, reduce heat, and simmer for 5 minutes. Stir occasionally and set aside.

For cornbread, combine corn flour and next 4 ingredients. Mix well. Stir in well drained chilies until coated. Add 1 cup cheese. Whisk together eggs, milk, and sour cream. Combine dry and wet mixtures until liquid is absorbed.

Spray 9x13 pan, and then pour in melted butter. Evenly spread cornbread mixture on top of butter, and then evenly spread meat on top of cornbread. Bake for 10 minutes, reduce heat to 350°, and bake another 20-25 minutes or until center is done. Sprinkle remaining cheese on top. Serve with your favorite taco toppings such as diced tomatoes, chopped onion, cilantro, avocado, black beans, sour cream, salsa, lettuce, and olives.

Serves 8

FROM THE PANTRY

1-2 pounds ground Italian sausage

1-2 chicken breasts, chopped

3 tablespoons olive oil, divided

1 medium onion, diced

3 stalks celery, chopped

8-ounce package mushrooms, chopped

3 cloves garlic, chopped

1 red pepper, chopped

3 cups cubed zucchini

3 cups cubed yellow squash

2 cups diced carrots

2 cups chopped fresh spinach

15.5-ounce can cannellini beans, drained

14.5-ounce can or 16-ounce frozen package Italian green beans

2 14.5-ounce cans diced tomatoes

2 tablespoons chopped fresh basil

2 teaspoons garlic powder

2 tablespoons Italian seasoning

4 cups chicken broth, plain or Tuscany

Italian Sausage Soup

This soup is a perfect expression of the kind of cook I am—a kitchen sink cook. Pretty much everything but the kitchen sink is in this beautiful blend of Italy meets the Deep South.

HOW TO CREATE

Brown sausage, drain, and set aside.

Sauté chicken in 1 tablespoon olive oil until pink disappears. Set aside.

In large pot, sauté next 5 ingredients in 2 tablespoons olive oil for 2 minutes. Add zucchini and yellow squash, and sauté for additional 2 minutes.

Add meat and remaining ingredients. Add salt and pepper to taste. Bring to low boil, and then simmer for 45 minutes, stirring occasionally. Top with Parmesan cheese.

Serves 15

chapter 4
CLASSY CARBS

Asking if cheese is gluten free is a common question. For most cheeses, the answer is yes. When in doubt, call customer service or go to the brand's website.

Macaroni and Cheese

After my first bite of this gourmet version of mac and cheese, I will never think of it the same again. Preparation is longer than opening a box, but it is worth every additional minute.

FROM THE PANTRY

8 ounces quinoa elbow pasta

2 tablespoons butter

2 tablespoons gluten-free all-purpose flour

2 cups milk

2 ounces shredded Gruyere cheese

8 ounces shredded white cheddar

2 tablespoons shredded Parmesan cheese

4 ounces shredded Fontina cheese

1 teaspoon smoked paprika

4 pieces bacon, crispy and crumbled

4 slices gluten-free bread

1 tablespoon melted butter

HOW TO CREATE

Preheat oven to 350°.

Prepare pasta according to directions (boil no longer than 9 minutes).

On medium high heat, whisk butter and flour in large saucepan. Add 1/2 cup milk and stir until sauce thickens. Continue whisking as you add additional 1/2 cup milk. When thickened add final cup milk and whisk until thickened again. Remove saucepan from heat and stir in four cheeses until completely blended. Add smoked paprika.

In a food processor, pulse bread slices into crumbs. Toss crumbs with melted butter, spread on baking sheet, and brown *lightly* in 400° oven. Time varies depending on oven, so watch carefully so they don't burn. Stir with fork after a few minutes, and then continue browning. Set aside.

Mix pasta and sauce, and then pour into 13x9 baking dish. Top with crispy, crumbled bacon and bread crumbs. Bake for 15 minutes.

Serves 6

Corn Muffins

Double the corn in these muffins with one of my favorite new discoveries, corn flour. A golden accompaniment to any entree, this muffin's smooth and light texture makes it flawless.

Pictured with the muffins is "Hope Street Bean Soup," which holds a special place in my stomach and heart! It can be purchased from Wildwood Church in Tallahassee, Florida, and the proceeds benefit children in Uganda.

FROM THE PANTRY

1 cup corn flour

3/4 cup yellow cornmeal

1 tablespoon sugar

1 teaspoon xanthan gum

2 teaspoons baking powder

1/2 teaspoon baking soda

1 teaspoon salt

2 eggs

1 cup buttermilk

1/4 cup oil

HOW TO CREATE

In large mixing bowl, combine all dry ingredients.

In medium bowl, combine milk, oil, and eggs.

Pour liquid into corn flour mixture, and stir vigorously to combine. Let dough rest for at least 15 minutes.

Preheat oven to 400°. Lightly oil 24-cup mini muffin tin or 12-cup regular muffin tin, and fill each cup 3/4 full. Bake for 12-15 minutes for mini muffins or 20-25 minutes for regular muffins. Check for doneness by pressing top of muffin.

Yields 24 mini muffins or 12 regular muffins

Delightful Dinner Rolls

Playing around in the kitchen trying to reproduce the old-fashioned mayonnaise biscuit gave birth to this delightful dinner roll. Heavy on the "light," these rolls are crispy on the outside and tender on the inside.

FROM THE PANTRY

2 cups white rice flour

1/2 cup tapioca flour

1 teaspoon xanthan gum

2 teaspoons baking powder

1 teaspoon salt

1 cup plus 2 tablespoons milk

3/4 cup Hellmann's mayonnaise

HOW TO CREATE

Whisk together dry ingredients.

In separate bowl, combine milk and mayonnaise. Fold into dry ingredients until flour is absorbed and no lumps remain, about 1 minute. Let dough rest for 15 minutes.

Preheat oven to 400°.

Lightly oil 24-cup mini muffin tin. With rounded scoop, divide dough evenly into muffin cups. Cups will be very full. Bake for 12-15 minutes. Cool on wire rack.

Yields 24 dinner rolls

Pumpkin Bread

Trick or treat? Nothing scary about this gluten-free pumpkin patch! Each pumpkin loaf is a creamy mixture of fall spices just waiting to be picked for the holiday season. It will surely be a real treat!

FROM THE PANTRY

1-1/2 cups brown rice flour

3/4 cup sweet sorghum flour

3/4 cup tapioca starch

2 teaspoons xanthan gum

2 teaspoons baking soda

1-1/2 teaspoons salt

1 teaspoon cinnamon

1 teaspoon nutmeg

3 cups sugar

1 cup oil

4 eggs

16-ounce can pumpkin

2/3 cup water

HOW TO CREATE

Preheat oven to 350°.

Sift or whisk together first 8 ingredients.

Cream sugar and oil, and then add eggs, pumpkin, and water.

Pour liquid mixture into dry ingredients and mix well. Pour batter into three lightly oiled 8-1/2x4-1/2 loaf pans and bake for 1 hour. Cool in pans for 5 minutes, and then transfer to wire rack.

Yields 3 loaves

This recipe is amazingly moist on its own, but if you want a little something extra, use your favorite cream cheese, caramel, or butter cream frosting.

Cornbread Dressing

Holidays are back to normal with this amazing "I can't believe it's gluten free" dressing. Based on our family's favorite recipe, this holiday tradition lives on!

Cornbread

FROM THE PANTRY

1 cup yellow cornmeal

1/2 cup white or brown rice flour

2 teaspoons baking powder

1 teaspoon xanthan gum

1 teaspoon salt

3/4 cup buttermilk

2 eggs

2 tablespoons oil

HOW TO CREATE

In large mixing bowl, combine first 5 ingredients. In separate bowl, combine last 3 ingredients.

Preheat oven to 350°.

Blend mixtures together and let rest for 15 minutes. Pour batter into 9x9 oiled pan. Bake for 20-25 minutes.

Dressing

FROM THE PANTRY

7 slices gluten-free bread, dried in oven

1 recipe corn bread (see above)

8-ounce package gluten-free stuffing

2 cups chopped celery

1 large onion, chopped

1 stick butter

8 cups chicken stock or broth

1 teaspoon salt

1/2 teaspoon pepper

1 heaping teaspoon sage

1 tablespoon poultry seasoning

5 eggs, beaten

HOW TO CREATE

In very large bowl, crumble bread and corn bread. Add stuffing.

Sauté celery and onion in butter for 3 minutes and pour over bread mixture.

Add salt, pepper, sage, and poultry seasoning.

Preheat oven to 350°.

Pour chicken stock over bread mixture. Add eggs, stir well, and let sit for 30 minutes to absorb liquid.

Pour into large 15x11 baking pan and bake for 45 minutes or until firm.

Serves 8-10

Stuffing Muffins

Revive your leftover dressing by making "Stuffing Muffins."
Complement them with "Cranberry Surprise," a flavorful fruit blend that is true to the season.

Muffins

FROM THE PANTRY

4 cups leftover gluten-free stuffing

1 cup chopped leftover turkey or chicken

1 egg, beaten

HOW TO CREATE

Preheat oven to 350°.

Combine all ingredients and mix well.

Oil 24-cup mini muffin tin and fill each cup 3/4 full.

Bake 25-30 minutes or until firm to touch. Transfer to serving dish.

Cranberry Surprise

FROM THE PANTRY

3 cups fresh cranberries (12-ounce package)

Zest from 2 oranges

2 oranges, peeled and seeded

3 apples, chopped

Juice from 1 lemon

2-1/2 cups sugar

1 tablespoon cornstarch or tapioca starch

1-2 tablespoons cold water

HOW TO CREATE

Puree oranges in food processor.

In saucepan, simmer fruits, zest, and sugar for 15-20 minutes.

Dissolve starch in cold water. Pour into fruit mixture and cook, stirring until thickened.

Serves 5-6

Pecan Praline Sweet Potatoes

Opposites attract. So pairing this sweet treat with salty ham makes a perfect couple any time of year.

FROM THE PANTRY

2 large sweet potatoes

1 cup pecans

1/4 cup sugar

1/2 cup sweet sorghum flour plus 3 tablespoons for rolling dough

6 tablespoons cold butter

PECAN PRALINES

1/2 cup sugar

3/4 cup brown sugar

1/2 cup heavy cream

1 tablespoon butter

1 teaspoon vanilla nut flavoring
(may substitute vanilla flavoring)

1 cup finely chopped pecans, divided

Combine sugars, cream, and butter in medium saucepan. Bring to low boil on medium high heat and stir for 1 minute.

Remove from heat and add vanilla nut flavoring and 3/4 cup pecans, reserving 1/4 cup for topping.

HOW TO CREATE

Preheat oven to 400°.

Wash and peel sweet potatoes. Chop into 1/2-inch squares and set aside in large mixing bowl.

To make crust, combine pecans, sugar, and 1/2 cup flour in food processor and pulse 6 times. Cut butter into 6 pieces and add to processor. Pulse mixture until butter is incorporated and soft dough forms.

Cover bottom of oiled 2-quart casserole dish or 9-inch springform pan with dough to form crust. Sprinkle 3 tablespoons flour on top of crust to prevent sticking as you spread dough 2 inches up side of pan.

Pour praline mixture (see at left) on top of sweet potatoes and mix thoroughly.

Pour sweet potato mixture into crust. Cover with foil and bake for 40 minutes. Add remaining 1/4 cup pecans to top of casserole and bake uncovered for additional 10 minutes. Cool and serve.

Serves 8-10

BACON, LETTUCE, *and*
Fried Green Tomatoes

Halfway to the studio for The Noon Show, I realized I would be frying green tomatoes in pearls and heels! Whoa ... a true southern girl! No matter where you are from, this crispy, breadless BLT is sure to complement any entrée!

FROM THE PANTRY

4 firm green tomatoes

1-1/4 cups corn flour (divided)

1 cup yellow cornmeal

2 teaspoons salt

2 eggs

2 teaspoons water

Refined coconut oil or extra light olive oil

8 bacon slices, crispy and broken
into tiny pieces

Shredded lettuce

1 cup mayonnaise

2-3 heaping teaspoons horseradish

HOW TO CREATE

Choose tomatoes that are very firm and green to pinkish green in color. Slice each into 1/2-inch slices. Measure 3/4 cup corn flour and put in small bowl. Whisk together eggs and water. Combine remaining corn flour (1/2 cup), cornmeal, and salt, and place on plate for dredging.

On medium heat, heat enough oil to cover bottom of heavy frying pan. In conveyer fashion, coat each slice in corn flour, dip both sides in eggs, and then dredge through corn flour and meal mixture. Lightly tap to remove excess flour coating and place in oil. Cook until golden brown, turning only once. Remove to cooling rack or to your mouth!

Mix mayonnaise and horseradish, and set aside
while tomatoes cool slightly.

Place slightly cooled tomatoes on top of bed of shredded lettuce. Place dollop of mayonnaise and horseradish sauce on top of each tomato and sprinkle with crispy bacon pieces.

Serves 5-6

Quinoa Noodles
WITH VEGETABLES

Doing math with a stir-fry: Add a meat and you have
more than a sidekick. Subtract the noodles and you have a side of veggies.
Either way, this dish is an elegant equation!

FROM THE PANTRY

8-ounce package quinoa linguini noodles

1 cup carrots, cut into thin strips

1 cup red and yellow peppers, cut into 1-inch strips

1 cup chopped broccoli

1 cup sliced mushrooms

3 scallion stems, chopped

3 garlic cloves, chopped

4 cups chopped kale, spinach, and/or chard

3 tablespoons olive oil

1 teaspoon garlic powder

2-3 tablespoons gluten-free soy sauce

HOW TO CREATE

Cook noodles according to directions on
package, drain, and set aside.

Sauté carrots for 2 minutes in oil.

Add next 5 vegetables. Stir-fry for 1-1/2 to
2 minutes, add greens, and stir-fry for
additional minute.

Add noodles and garlic powder. Toss and
continue to stir-fry for additional minute.
Add 2-3 tablespoons soy sauce, or adjust
amount to taste.

Serves 6-8

Baked Green Bean Medley

Funny how adding a green bean to your meal can give you a sense of well-being. Sort of takes away the guilt when you haven't had quite enough veggies. Mixing the beans with mushrooms, onions, and a splash of liquid aminos makes this a side you'll add more often.

Cover the baking sheet with foil to reduce cleanup.

FROM THE PANTRY

1 pound fresh whole green beans

2 cups sliced white mushrooms

1 medium onion, thinly sliced

4 garlic cloves, sliced

1 teaspoon parsley

1/4 cup olive oil

2 tablespoons Liquid Aminos

Salt and pepper to taste

HOW TO CREATE

Preheat oven to 425°.

Cover large baking sheet with foil.

Rinse green beans and mushrooms, drain, and place in large bowl. Combine with onion, garlic, parsley, oil, and Liquid Aminos. Toss to coat thoroughly.

Transfer to large baking sheet and spread into single layer. Stirring once, bake for 20 minutes or until tender.

Serves 6

Vanilla Bean Crepes
WITH LEMON GLAZED FRUIT

It was sheer success when these delicate vanilla sensations took shape. Count the first one as practice, toss it, and then continue until your plate is brimming with this light and fruit-filled pancake.

FROM THE PANTRY

2 eggs, slightly beaten

1-3/4 cups milk

2 tablespoons oil

1/8 teaspoon vanilla flavoring

1 vanilla bean or additional 1/2 teaspoon vanilla flavoring

3/4 cup gluten-free all-purpose flour

1/4 teaspoon salt

2 tablespoons organic sugar

1 cup quartered and sliced strawberries

1 cup quartered and sliced bananas

1 cup blueberries

Confectioners' sugar

HOW TO CREATE

In medium bowl, whisk eggs, milk, oil, and flavoring. Split vanilla bean, scrape seeds into egg mixture, and mix well. If you don't have a vanilla bean, add 1/2 teaspoon vanilla flavoring. Add flour, salt, and sugar. Mix batter until smooth with whisk, blender, or hand mixer. Cover and rest batter for 1 hour. You may store batter in refrigerator for up to 48 hours.

With paper towel, wipe bottom of 6-inch frying or crepe pan with oil. On medium heat, drop 2 heaping tablespoons of batter in pan. Quickly spread batter with spatula, rolling pan to form a thin circle. When top is firm, flip crepe, and lightly brown. Place on plate and repeat with remaining batter.

For lemon glaze, boil water and sugar for 4 minutes. Set aside to cool, and then add lemon juice. In medium bowl, toss fruit with lemon glaze. Place 2 tablespoons of fruit mixture in middle of crepe and fold sides over fruit. Sprinkle with confectioners' sugar.

Yields approximately 12 crepes

LEMON GLAZE
1 cup water

3/4 cup organic sugar

Juice from 1 lemon

To obtain the vanilla seeds, split the vanilla bean pod lengthwise and scrape. Vanilla beans are expensive and can be substituted with an extra teaspoon of liquid vanilla.

Coconut Mango Muffins

Take your taste buds on a tropical vacation with these nutritious muffins. The four flours bring all the flavors together to make this sunny treat.

Using a wide-mouth canning funnel makes the coconut topping easy to apply.

FROM THE PANTRY

3/4 cup coconut sugar

1/3 cup coconut oil

2 eggs

2 large or 3 small mangos

1/2 cup coconut flour

1/2 cup white rice flour

1/2 cup brown rice flour

1/4 cup tapioca flour

2 teaspoons baking powder

1 teaspoon xanthan gum

1/2 teaspoon salt

3 tablespoons dry powdered milk

1 cup coconut, toasted

4.5 ounces macadamia nuts

3 tablespoons coconut sugar

HOW TO CREATE

Cream 3/4 cup sugar and oil. Add eggs and mix until blended.

Using food processor, chop mangos and add to sugar mixture.

In separate bowl, whisk dry ingredients together. Add dry ingredients to wet ingredients and mix on low for 1 minute. Allow batter to rest for 20 minutes while coconut is toasting.

For topping, toast coconut for 10 minutes in 170° oven.

Preheat oven to 375°. Chop nuts into small pieces and add 3 tablespoons sugar and toasted coconut.

Using small scoop, spoon dough into each cup of lightly oiled mini muffin tins. Top each with 1/2 teaspoon nut topping. Press topping down into dough. Bake for 15-18 minutes.

Yields 36 mini muffins

Ham and Spinach Strata

It's not a folded egg with filling—an omelet. It's not an unfolded egg with toppings—a frittata. It's a strata! Repeated layers of deliciousness with eggs, meat, vegetables, bread, and cheese.

FROM THE PANTRY

2 tablespoons olive oil

1 red pepper, chopped

1 yellow pepper, chopped

6 cups chopped fresh spinach

1 teaspoon salt, divided

1/4 teaspoon pepper

6 large eggs

1 cup milk

1/2 cup sour cream

8 slices gluten-free bread

8-10 ounces goat cheese

2 cups chopped ham

1 cup shredded Monterey jack cheese

HOW TO CREATE

Preheat oven to 350°.

Line 9-inch round or square springform pan with foil. Spray with cooking spray and set aside.

In Dutch oven on medium heat, add oil, spinach, and 1/2 teaspoon salt, and sauté until spinach wilts. Remove to colander to drain and cool. In same Dutch oven, sauté peppers for 1 minute. Drain and set aside to cool.

In medium bowl, whisk together eggs, milk, sour cream, pepper, and remaining 1/2 teaspoon salt.

Layer 4 slices of bread, half the goat cheese, half the ham, half the spinach, and half the peppers. Slowly pour half the egg mixture over first layer. Repeat with remaining bread, goat cheese, ham, spinach, and peppers. Top with Monterey jack cheese. Pour remaining egg mixture over cheese.

Refrigerate overnight or for at least 1 hour. When ready to bake, remove from refrigerator and bring to room temperature. Bake for 1 hour or until set. Cool strata for 15 minutes before serving.

Adding a 9-inch square springform pan to my collection was perfect for making this strata!

Serves 6-8

Peachy Pecan Pastry

When peaches and pecans get together, they produce the proof that living with a gluten issue can be positive!

This is one of the oldest gadgets in my kitchen! A wedding gift from my mom, it is an essential tool for making pastries and pie crusts!

FROM THE PANTRY

1 cup gluten-free
all-purpose flour

1/2 cup tapioca starch

1/2 cup sugar

2-1/2 teaspoons
baking powder

1/2 teaspoon baking soda

1/2 teaspoon salt

1/2 teaspoon xanthan gum

1/2 cup cold butter

2 tablespoons refined
coconut oil

1 cup sour cream

1 egg

1 teaspoon vanilla extract

2 peaches, peeled and diced small

1/2 cup chopped pecans, toasted

1 cup confectioners' sugar

1/2 teaspoon vanilla extract

2 tablespoons milk

Peach Delight by Mario Camacho Foods or peach preserves for garnishing

HOW TO CREATE

Combine first 7 ingredients and mix thoroughly. Using pastry blender, cut in cold butter and coconut oil until very small pieces form.

In separate bowl, mix sour cream, egg, 1 teaspoon vanilla extract, and peaches. Add to flour mixture and stir well. Spread dough evenly in 11-inch tart pan or 10-inch springform pan. Sprinkle toasted pecans on top. Let dough rest while oven is preheating.

Preheat oven to 375°. Bake tart for 40-50 minutes. Combine confectioners' sugar, 1/2 teaspoon vanilla, and milk, and drizzle on top of cooled tart. Garnish with *Peach Delight* or your favorite preserves.

Serves 10-12

CHERRY FILLING

12 ounces frozen cherries

1/4 cup tapioca starch/flour

1/3 cup sugar

1 teaspoon vanilla extract

Chop cherries into small pieces. In medium saucepan, heat cherries, starch/flour, and sugar on medium high heat. Stir constantly until thickened, approximately 10-15 minutes.

Remove from heat, add vanilla extract, and cool.

Almond Coffee Cake
WITH CHERRY CREAM CHEESE FILLING

Fact or fiction, George Washington's cherry tree story remains alive. It has been a character builder for children for many years. The truth is the cherry comes to life in this scrumptious coffee cake and was featured in a segment on George Washington's birthday!

CREAM CHEESE FILLING

8 ounces cream cheese, softened at room temperature

1/3 cup sugar

1 egg

Combine cream cheese, sugar, and egg, and beat well.

Coffee Cake Batter

FROM THE PANTRY

1-1/4 cups almond flour

1 cup sweet sorghum flour

3/4 cup sugar

1/4 cup tapioca starch/flour

3/4 cup cold butter

1 teaspoon xanthan gum

1/2 teaspoon baking powder

1/2 teaspoon baking soda

1/2 teaspoon salt

3/4 cup sour cream

1 egg

1-1/2 teaspoons almond extract

1 cup slivered almonds, divided

HOW TO CREATE

Preheat oven to 350°.

Mix flours, sugar, and starch/flour. Place in food processor, add cold butter slices, and pulse until mixture is crumbly. Remove 1 cup of crumbled mixture and set aside for topping.

Add xanthan gum, baking powder, baking soda, and salt to food processor, and pulse 5-6 more times. Place crumbled mixture in large mixing bowl.

In separate bowl, combine sour cream, egg, and almond extract. Add to crumbled mixture and mix well. In lightly oiled 9-inch springform pan, spread batter on bottom and up 2 inches of sides to form bottom layer. Place 1/2 cup almonds on top of batter.

ASSEMBLE

To assemble coffee cake, pour cream cheese mixture over batter. Spoon cherry filling on top of cream cheese mixture. Top with reserved crumb mixture and remaining 1/2 cup almonds.

Bake for 55-60 minutes. Remove sides of pan, cool, and store in refrigerator.

Serves 10-12

Date Nut Puffs

Light and airy, these puffs of confection melt in your mouth and send you back for more.

FROM THE PANTRY

3/4 cup white rice flour

1/4 cup tapioca flour

1 teaspoon baking powder

1 teaspoon xanthan gum

1/8 teaspoon salt

1 cup chopped dates

1 cup chopped walnuts

3 egg whites

1 cup sugar

1/4 teaspoon lemon zest

1/2 teaspoon vanilla extract

HOW TO CREATE

Preheat oven to 350°.

Combine flours, baking powder, xanthan gum, and salt. Add dates and walnuts. Mix thoroughly.

In clean, dry mixing bowl, beat egg whites with clean, dry beaters until foamy. Add sugar and beat until stiff peaks form to make a meringue. Add lemon zest and vanilla extract, and mix gently, just to combine.

Gently fold flour mixture into meringue. Drop by teaspoons onto lightly greased cookie sheet. Bake 8-10 minutes. Cool on wire rack.

Yields 4 dozen puffs

Granola

From an old southern plantation, this recipe yields lots of sweet goodness. Pair it with fruit and yogurt to make a beautiful work of art.

FROM THE PANTRY

4 cups gluten-free oats

1/2 cup ground flax seed

1/2 cup coconut

1/2 cup chopped pecans or walnuts

1/2 cup sesame seeds

1/2 cup sunflower seeds

1/2 cup slivered or chopped almonds

1/2 cup chopped dates

3/4 cup raisins, golden and/or brown

1/2 cup vegetable or coconut oil

1 cup honey

HOW TO CREATE

Preheat oven to 350°.

Mix together first 7 ingredients and spread evenly on baking pan.

Bake until lightly browned, stirring every 5 minutes. This may take 20-25 minutes; be very careful not to overcook.

When mixture is browned, pour into large bowl and add dates and raisins. In microwave or on top of stove, heat oil and honey until very warm. Toss oat mixture with oil and honey.

Yields 8 cups; serve as a cereal with milk or as a topping on yogurt, ice cream, fruit, etc.

HELPFUL HINTS

Store in an airtight container in the pantry. For longer storage, move to refrigerator or freezer.

Oats are naturally gluten free. But if you have celiac disease, oats labeled gluten free are recommended because of the possibility of cross contamination in unlabeled brands.

Blueberry Custard Tartlets

I'll do anything to be with my incredible family, including picking tiny berries under a blazing hot sun in bushes where snakes may be crawling. With all the laughter, chatting, and sweating, filling a gallon bucket with these plump and tasty indigo berries is no problem—unless you're 2 and your name is Scotlyn Grace. Her system was simple: four in the bucket, four back out and into her mouth. Needless to say, Scotlyn Grace's bucket was empty by the end of our family adventure.

FROM THE PANTRY

3 cups fresh blueberries

4 tablespoons tapioca starch

2 eggs

Lemon zest

1 cup sugar

1 tablespoon lemon juice

1 tablespoon butter

1 cup finely ground almonds

1 cup coconut flour

1 teaspoon xanthan gum

4 tablespoons coconut oil

1/2 cup coconut sugar

2 eggs, lightly beaten

3 tablespoons milk

HOW TO CREATE

To make custard, puree blueberries with tapioca starch and lemon juice. In saucepan, whisk together eggs, lemon zest, and sugar. Add pureed blueberry mixture and cook over medium high heat stirring constantly until thickened. Take off burner, add butter, and set aside to cool.

Preheat oven to 375°. To make crust, pulse almonds until very fine. Combine with flour and xanthan gum. In separate bowl, combine oil, sugar, eggs, and milk, and add to flour mixture. Place 3-4 teaspoons of dough in each cup of mini muffin tin. Press dough to cover bottom and sides.

Bake for 8-10 minutes. Cool 2-3 minutes, and then carefully remove to cooling rack and fill with blueberry custard.

Top tartlets with frosting using small scoop or decorating bag with tip.

Yields 36 tartlets

FROSTING

4 ounces cream cheese

1 tablespoon lemon juice

4 tablespoons heavy cream

4 cups confectioners' sugar

Combine and mix thoroughly cream cheese, lemon juice, cream, and confectioners' sugar.

Zesty Chocolate Scones

Friends share their lives with you. Really good friends share their recipes—which makes this one very special.

FROM THE PANTRY

1 cup white rice flour

1/2 cup sweet sorghum flour

1/2 cup tapioca starch

1 teaspoon xanthan gum

1/3 cup sugar

1 tablespoon baking powder

1/2 teaspoon salt

1/2 cup mini chocolate chips (chocolate lovers add more)

Zest from one large orange

1-1/4 cups heavy cream, plus additional to form soft dough

HOW TO CREATE

Combine dry ingredients with whisk. Add chocolate chips and orange zest.

Add heavy cream and mix with fork for 1 minute adding additional cream if needed. Let dough rest for 10 minutes.

Preheat oven to 425°. Using white rice flour, lightly flour sheet of parchment paper. Place dough on paper and form into ball. Lightly knead and pat dough to 3/4-inch thickness.

Brush top of dough with cream and sprinkle with sugar. Depending on the occasion, you may use different colored sugars: pink, red, green, etc.

With floured cookie cutter or knife, cut into shapes you desire. Transfer scones to lightly oiled parchment paper and bake for 12-15 minutes.

Yields 1 dozen 2-inch scones

Figs in a Blanket

The fig. You either love it or you don't.
The truth is my love for it grew because it's the only
fruit-bearing tree that has ever survived my non-green thumb.
It produces wildly, leaving me with lots and lots of vitamin
pumped fruit and inspiring me to create sumptuous figgy recipes.

Pastry

FROM THE PANTRY

1-1/4 cups white rice flour

3/4 cup tapioca starch

3/4 cup sugar

1 teaspoon xanthan gum

1/2 teaspoon salt

2 teaspoons baking powder

1/2 cup butter flavored shortening

2/3 cup heavy cream (may substitute with another milk product)

1 egg

1-1/2 teaspoons vanilla extract

HOW TO CREATE

Whisk together first 6 ingredients in large mixing bowl. With pastry cutter, cut shortening into flour mixture until it forms fine crumbs.

In small mixing bowl, mix cream, egg, and vanilla extract. Add to crumb mixture, folding together with spatula until completely mixed. Continue mixing for another minute. Let dough rest for 15 minutes.

Preheat oven to 375°. Cover large cookie sheet with parchment paper. Oil and flour paper with any gluten-free flour. Place dough in center of paper and form into 14x10 rectangle.

Place fig filling in middle of dough, leaving at least 3 inches on each side. Cut dough into 2-inch wide strips on each side and gently fold strips over fig filling. The dough is delicate. If it breaks, press it back together. Bake for 30 minutes or until lightly browned. Cool and transfer to serving dish.

Serves 10-12

*Petite Sallie Catherine
and my giant fig tree*

FIG FILLING

2 cups fresh figs

1/2-1 cup sugar (use more
or less to suit your taste)

In saucepan, mash figs
with sugar and cook
on medium heat until
thickened, approximately
45 minutes, stirring
often.

Set fig filling
aside to cool.

GLAZE

1 cup
confectioners' sugar

1-2 tablespoons milk

1/4 teaspoon
vanilla extract

Combine confectioners'
sugar, milk, and
vanilla extract.

Drizzle over
cooled pastry.

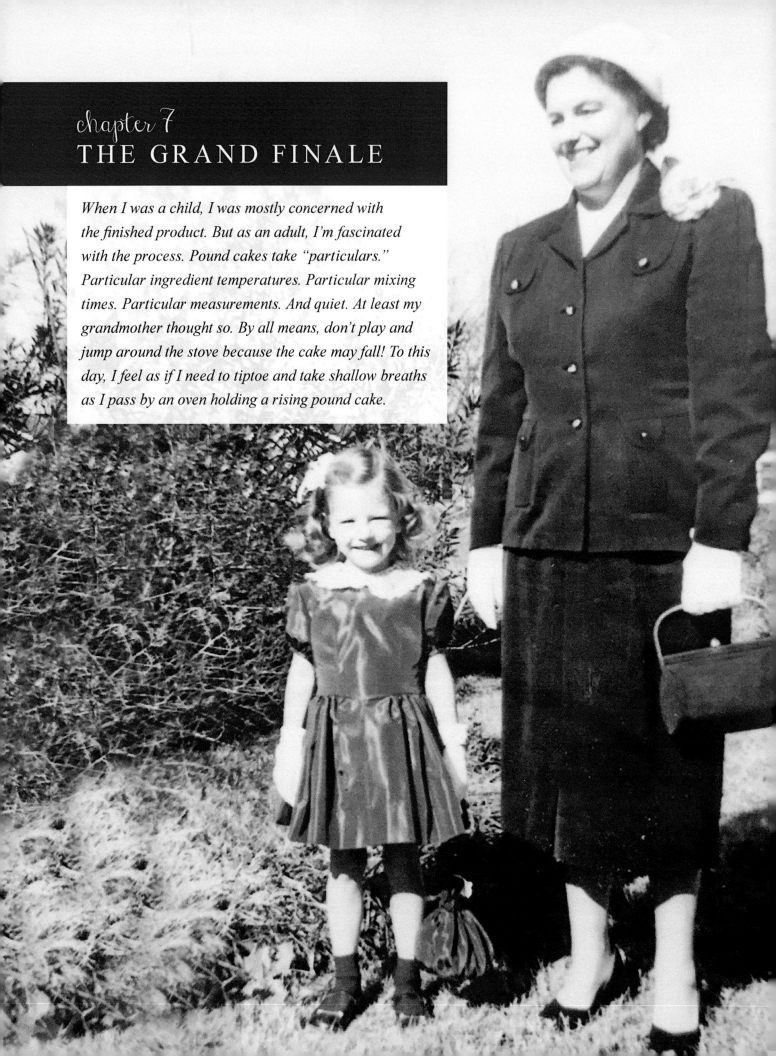

chapter 7
THE GRAND FINALE

When I was a child, I was mostly concerned with the finished product. But as an adult, I'm fascinated with the process. Pound cakes take "particulars." Particular ingredient temperatures. Particular mixing times. Particular measurements. And quiet. At least my grandmother thought so. By all means, don't play and jump around the stove because the cake may fall! To this day, I feel as if I need to tiptoe and take shallow breaths as I pass by an oven holding a rising pound cake.

Lemon Cream Cheese Pound Cake

Nothing says "my grandmother" like a pound cake. A real southern beauty with a peachy cream complexion, my grandmother's pound cakes rose to perfection, were crowned with a crispy crust, and had a melt in your mouth texture. Our family crest should have a picture of a pound cake on it. It's family nostalgia, history, and love in a tube pan. Not being able to imagine life without my grandmother's pound cake sent me on a creative quest for this family heirloom. This is one of the first recipes I reinvented and the first to air on WCTV, in 2012.

FROM THE PANTRY

2 sticks butter, softened at room temperature

1/2 cup shortening

8 ounces cream cheese, softened at room temperature

2-1/2 cups sugar

6 eggs, room temperature

Zest from 2 lemons

Juice from 1 lemon

1 teaspoon vanilla extract

1-1/2 cups white rice flour

1 cup sweet sorghum flour

1/2 cup potato starch

1 teaspoon baking powder

1 teaspoon xanthan gum

HOW TO CREATE

Preheat oven to 300°.

In mixing bowl, beat butter and shortening for 2 minutes.
Add cream cheese and continue to beat for 1 more minute.
Add sugar slowly and cream for 5-6 minutes until mixture is light and fluffy.

Add eggs one at a time, mixing after each addition. Add zest, lemon juice, and vanilla extract.

Combine all dry ingredients and whisk together. With mixer on low, slowly add dry ingredients to creamed mixture 1/2 cup at a time. Pour batter evenly into lightly oiled and floured tube pan. Run knife through batter to remove air bubbles. Bake for 1-1/4 to 1-1/2 hours or until toothpick inserted near center comes out clean. Cool cake in pan on wire rack for 10 minutes. Remove cake from pan and continue cooling on wire rack.

Serves 12-15

Butterscotch Apple Pie

My kitchen counter with its baking ingredients is my artist's palette. It's here where the creativity begins and one of the places I feel most alive. It was on one such occasion that this Butterscotch Apple Pie began to take shape—literally. Instead of the traditional apple placement, I stood each apple slice straight up, round and round until the bottom of the crust was covered, adding a sprinkling of butterscotch morsels for the finishing touch.

FROM THE PANTRY

1 cup white rice flour

1/2 cup brown rice flour

1/2 cup tapioca starch

1/2 teaspoon salt

1 teaspoon xanthan gum

1/2 cup chilled shortening

1 egg

3 tablespoons cold water

9-10 apples

4 tablespoons butter

5 tablespoons cornstarch

1/2 cup sugar

1-3/4 cups butterscotch morsels, divided

Serves 10-12

This wooden double rolling pin fits easily inside a pan for rolling a crust.

HOW TO CREATE

Preheat oven to 375°.

In food processor, pulse first 5 ingredients to combine. Add shortening and pulse until blended. Whisk egg with water and add to flour blend. Pulse until dough forms into a ball. Separate 3/4 cup dough for crumb topping. Place remaining dough in lightly oiled springform pan and press evenly on bottom and halfway up sides to form a crust.

Wash, core, and slice apples into 8 slices each. Place sliced apples standing long side up in a circle starting on the outside and working your way into the middle with smaller and smaller circles. Melt butter and drizzle over apples.

Place cornstarch, sugar, and 3/4 cup butterscotch morsels in food processor, pulsing mixture into fine powder. Sprinkle butterscotch mixture over and between apples. Put remaining 3/4 cup dough in food processor and pulse enough to make small crumbs. Sprinkle on top of apples.

Lightly cover top with foil and bake for 30 minutes. Uncover pie, reduce oven temperature to 350°, and bake for additional 20 minutes or until apples are tender.

As soon as pie is done, sprinkle remaining 1 cup morsels over apples. Cool in pan on wire rack for 20 minutes, and then remove side of springform pan.

Brownie With Espresso Meringue

If you want a new friend, just hang out on the grocery store chocolate aisle. If you want a triple chocolate shock, then this is sure to satisfy!

CAKE BROWNIE

3/4 cup butter

1-1/4 cups sugar

3/4 cup unsweetened cocoa, either special dark, original, or blend of both

2 eggs

1 teaspoon vanilla extract

1-1/4 cups brown rice flour

1/2 cup tapioca flour

1 teaspoon xanthan gum

1 teaspoon baking powder

1/4 teaspoon baking soda

1 cup milk

Preheat oven to 350°.

Cream butter and sugar until light and fluffy. On low speed add cocoa 1/4 cup at a time. When combined, increase mixer speed to medium high and beat for 3 minutes. Reduce mixer speed and add eggs and vanilla extract. Mix and set aside.

Combine flours, xanthan gum, baking powder, and soda. Alternating flour mixture with milk, add both to chocolate batter, beating well after each addition. Pour batter into 10x10 lightly oiled baking pan. Bake for 25-30 minutes or until middle is firm. Cool in pan on wire rack.

FROSTING

1 cup milk chocolate chips

1 cup confectioners' sugar

1/4 cup butter

1/4 cup milk

Combine all ingredients in medium saucepan on medium heat and stir until mixture forms fudge-like consistency.

Frost cooled brownies. Cut brownies into bite-sized squares and remove to plate.

If instant espresso coffee is hard to find, use instant coffee.

ESPRESSO MERINGUE

3 tablespoons instant espresso coffee

1/3 cup hot water

1 cup sugar

1 teaspoon vanilla extract

3 egg whites (room temperature)

1/4 teaspoon cream of tartar

1 cup morsels, any flavor, melted for drizzling

Combine espresso, water, and sugar in medium saucepan and bring mixture to boil. Boil for 2 minutes, and then remove from stove and add vanilla extract.

In separate clean, dry bowl with clean, dry beaters, beat egg whites until frothy, add cream of tartar, and beat until stiff peaks form. With mixer on low, slowly add espresso syrup and continue beating another 3 minutes.

In a trifle bowl, alternate layers of brownies and meringue starting with brownies and finishing with layer of meringue. Drizzle melted morsels on top.

Serves 10-12

Vanilla Pear Dessert

My childhood home always had a sand pear tree. This very hard fruit would give you a concussion if one fell on your head. My brother and his wife carry on the tradition of preserving these delicious fruits by having an assembly line pear party every year. If it can't be fun ...

FROM THE PANTRY

4 cups chopped pears (4-6 pears)

3 tablespoons cornstarch

1 cup white morsels

3/4 cup white rice flour

1/4 cup tapioca flour

1-1/2 teaspoons baking powder

1/4 teaspoon salt

1 teaspoon xanthan gum

4 tablespoons sugar, divided

1/4 cup cold butter

1 vanilla bean, optional

1 cup milk

1-1/2 teaspoons vanilla extract

1 egg

HOW TO CREATE

Preheat oven to 400°.

Peel, slice thin, and chop pears into very small pieces. Mix pears with cornstarch and morsels. Place pear mixture in lightly oiled 9x13 baking dish.

In separate bowl, mix next 5 ingredients and 2 tablespoons sugar. With pastry cutter, cut in cold butter.

Optional: Cut 1 stem of vanilla bean down the middle, scrape seeds into dry mix, and mix well.

Combine milk, vanilla extract, and egg. Pour into dry mixture, mix well, and spread over pears. Sprinkle 2 tablespoons sugar on top and bake for 30-35 minutes or until golden brown.

Serves 10-12

Creamy Coconut Filled Cookies

Rich in every way, these are meant to be eaten very slowly so as to capture every flavor. They're also meant to be shared. You'll make new best friends every time!

Cookie Pastry

FROM THE PANTRY

1 cup butter, softened at room temperature

1-1/2 cups sugar

2 eggs

1 teaspoon vanilla extract

1 teaspoon cream of tartar

1 teaspoon baking soda

1 teaspoon xanthan gum

1/4 teaspoon salt

1 cup coconut flour

1 cup white rice flour

1/2 cup tapioca starch

HOW TO CREATE

Cream butter and sugar for 5 minutes. Add eggs and vanilla extract, and mix until combined.

Mix together all dry ingredients and slowly add 1/2 cup at a time to creamed mixture. Divide in half and press each half into two lightly greased 10x15 pans. Set aside.

Yields 40-50 cookies

Coconut Filling and Topping

FROM THE PANTRY

3/4 cup butter

1 cup sugar

1 cup light corn syrup

14 ounces sweetened condensed milk

1 teaspoon vanilla extract

8 cups toasted coconut

1 cup chocolate chips, milk, dark, or semi-sweet

HOW TO CREATE

Preheat oven to 375°.

Combine coconut, butter, sugar, syrup, milk, and vanilla extract. Divide mixture between pans and bake for 12-15 minutes. Cool slightly.

Melt chocolate chips and drizzle on top. Cut into squares when cool.

HOW TO TOAST COCONUT

Preheat oven to 325°.

Spread coconut in even layer on baking sheet.

Heat in oven for about 10 minutes, stirring often. Watch carefully so coconut doesn't burn.

Save leftover bread pieces in a freezer bag in the freezer to use in bread puddings or to turn into bread crumbs.

German Chocolate Bread Pudding

Group gatherings are a great place to get new gluten-free food ideas. This luscious bread pudding recipe was inspired by a lovely dessert all my gluten-eating friends were raving about. I tweaked it here and there, made it gluten free, and now I can have my bread pudding and eat it, too.

FROM THE PANTRY

1 cup semi-sweet chocolate chips

1/2 cup brown sugar

1/4 cup butter, plus 1 tablespoon

1 cup milk

2 eggs

1 tablespoon vanilla extract

1 teaspoon instant espresso powder

1/4 teaspoon salt

1/2 pound gluten-free bread chopped into small cubes (sandwich, hamburger, hot dog, or baguettes)

HOW TO CREATE

Preheat oven to 350°.

Coat 9-inch springform pan with 1 tablespoon butter. In medium saucepan, melt chocolate chips with sugar and 1/4 cup butter, stirring frequently over low heat until mixture is smooth.

Whisk milk, eggs, vanilla extract, espresso, and salt together, and pour over bread cubes. Toss well so bread absorbs most of the liquid. Fold melted chocolate into bread mixture, and then transfer to prepared pan.

Bake for 50 minutes or until center springs back when gently pressed. (While pudding bakes, prepare sauce as directed at right.) Cool on rack for 20 minutes, remove sides of pan, top with sauce, and slice. Double recipe for more servings.

Yields 10-12 slices

SAUCE

2 tablespoons butter

1/2 cup brown sugar

1/2 cup heavy cream

1 egg yolk

Pinch of salt

1/4 cup chopped pecans, toasted

1/4 cup coconut, toasted

Melt butter and sugar in small saucepan over medium heat. Stir in cream, yolk, and salt. Boil for 1 minute or until slightly thickened.

Remove from heat and add pecans and coconut. Cool to room temperature and pour over bread pudding.

Peachy Cream Dessert

This is a great make-ahead dessert!

Living in the panhandle of Florida, we have access to the freshest variety of vegetables and fruits. Our neighboring state of Georgia harvests the sweetest peaches ever, and when this much anticipated season rolls around it is sure to stimulate the need for new ways to enjoy this juicy fruit. This Peachy Cream Dessert came to life on one such occasion.

FROM THE PANTRY

5 cups Vanilla Chex cereal

1/2 cup butter, melted

6 peaches

Juice from 1 lemon

8 ounces cream cheese, softened at room temperature

1-3/4 cups sugar, divided

1 teaspoon vanilla extract

2 cups heavy cream

1 package Knox gelatin

1/4 cup water

Serves 10-12

HOW TO CREATE

Preheat oven to 350°.

In food processor, finely chop cereal, add melted butter, and pulse to combine. Press into lightly oiled springform pan, covering bottom and halfway up side of pan to form a crust. Bake for 10 minutes. Cool completely on wire rack.

Peel and slice peaches top to bottom into 8 slices each. Gently toss sliced peaches with lemon juice. Place layer of peach slices on top of cooled crust, approximately 16 slices.

Beat cream cheese and 1 cup sugar thoroughly. Add vanilla extract.

In large mixing bowl, whip cream until stiff peaks form. Combine with cream cheese mixture. Finely chop 8 peach slices and fold into cream cheese mixture. Pour over crust and peach slices.

In food processor, puree 8 peach slices and add 3/4 cup sugar. Bring pureed mixture to boil in saucepan. In medium bowl, sprinkle gelatin on top of 1/4 cup water to dissolve. Pour hot mixture into gelatin and stir to combine. Set aside to cool. Place remaining peach slices on top of cream cheese layer and cover with peach gelatin. Refrigerate until firm, 8-12 hours.

Peanut Butter Cup Cake

There is nothing like quick and simple when you have time constraints and little ones pulling at your legs. This is a fun dessert that the kids can help with!

To date, my favorite two-layer cake mix is King Arthur.

Not all peanut butter cups are gluten free. The brand I use is Reese's.

FROM THE PANTRY

Two-layer gluten-free yellow cake mix

Additional ingredients on back of box

12 ounces Reese's Peanut Butter Cups

1 cup creamy peanut butter

4-5 cups confectioners' sugar

1/2-3/4 cup milk

HOW TO CREATE

Preheat oven to 350°.

Prepare cake according to package directions. Pour batter into lightly oiled 9x13 pan. Unwrap peanut butter cups and place randomly in cake mix. Lightly spread cake mix over peanut butter cups. Bake for 40-45 minutes. Cool completely in pan on wire rack.

For frosting, cream together 1 cup any gluten-free peanut butter and 1/2 cup milk. Slowly add 3 cups confectioners' sugar. After mixing well, add another cup confectioners' sugar. To achieve desired consistency, add additional milk and/or sugar. Spread frosting on cooled cake.

Serves 15-20

Nutella Brownies

The first of six grandchildren, Elizabeth Williamson loves her Nutella! And yes, Nutella is gluten free! This hazelnut blend of creaminess came into being in Italy during World War II as the result of a chocolate shortage. Just another example of "necessity is the mother of invention." Today it has evolved into a household staple, has a variety of uses, and was born to be paired with the ever loved brownie!

FROM THE PANTRY

1/2 cup butter, softened at room temperature

3/4 cup sugar

3/4 cup (6 ounces) Nutella

4 eggs

1 teaspoon vanilla flavoring or hazelnut flavoring

1 cup white rice flour

1/2 cup tapioca starch

1/2 teaspoon salt

1 teaspoon baking powder

1 teaspoon xanthan gum

1/2 cup chopped hazelnuts or walnuts

Optional frosting: 1/2 cup Nutella, 3 tablespoons hazelnut creamer

HOW TO CREATE

Cream butter and sugar for 5 minutes or longer, until light and fluffy. Add Nutella and continue to beat until well combined. Add eggs one at a time, beating after each addition. Add flavoring.

Mix together flour, starch, salt, baking powder, and xanthan gum. On lowest speed of mixer, add flour mixture 1/2 cup at a time. Add nuts. Mix until blended, and then let batter rest for 15 minutes.

Preheat oven to 350°. Oil 10x10 or similar size pan. Pour brownie mixture into pan and bake for 25-30 minutes or until firm on top.

Cool on wire rack, slice, and top with frosting (optional).

Serves 25-30

These brownies are so moist they are very good without frosting. But if you would like more of the hazelnut flavor, combine 1/2 cup Nutella with 3 tablespoons hazelnut flavored coffee creamer. Drizzle over the cooled brownies and top with chopped hazelnuts.

Cookie Cream Dessert
BETTER KNOWN AS "DIRT"

Not to be undone by gluten, substitute a gluten-free chocolate cookie to bring this well-known dessert back to your table.

FROM THE PANTRY

1/4 cup butter, softened at room temperature

8 ounces cream cheese

1 cup confectioners' sugar

3-1/2 cups milk

2 3.9-ounce boxes French vanilla instant pudding

12 ounces frozen whipped topping

10.6-ounce package gluten-free chocolate cream-filled cookies *(pictured, Glutino brand)*

HOW TO CREATE

Cream butter and cream cheese. Add confectioners' sugar and mix for at least 3 minutes.

In another bowl, combine pudding and milk and mix for 2 minutes. After pudding begins to thicken, add whipped topping and mix well. Combine cream cheese and pudding mixtures thoroughly.

In food processor, pulse cookies until they look like dirt. Place layer of cookie crumbs on bottom of container, and then add layer of creamed mixture. Continue to alternate layers finishing with cookie crumbs on top. Refrigerate.

Suggestions for serving this old family favorite are trifle bowls, individual serving bowls, or clay flower pots. You can decorate with fake flowers and top with a few gummy worms.

Serves 12-15

Fruit Pizza

Fruit with a delicate cookie crust enhanced by cream cheese and white morsels is a beautiful centerpiece for any occasion. Unless you have a comedic cousin like mine—all he can see is a dart board. One thing for sure, you will surely hit the target with this great tasting and healthy dessert!

FROM THE PANTRY

3/4 cup butter, softened at room temperature

1/2 cup confectioners' sugar

1/2 cup almond flour

3/4 cup white rice flour

1/4 tapioca flour

1 teaspoon xanthan gum

12 ounces white morsels

1/4 cup heavy whipping cream

8 ounces cream cheese, softened at room temperature

1 pint fresh strawberries, sliced

1 pint fresh blueberries

3 kiwifruit, peeled and sliced

1 pint fresh pineapple, cut into small pieces

4 tablespoons sugar

3 teaspoons cornstarch

1/8-1/4 cup reserved pineapple juice

1 teaspoon lemon juice

HOW TO CREATE

Preheat oven to 325°.

Cream together butter and confectioners' sugar until light and fluffy. In separate bowl, mix flours and xanthan gum, and then slowly add to creamed mixture to form cookie dough. Press dough into lightly greased 12-inch pizza pan. Bake for 20-25 minutes or until lightly browned. Cool completely on wire rack.

Melt morsels in microwave on high, stirring well after 30-second intervals. Transfer to mixing bowl and combine melted morsels and whipping cream. Add cream cheese and mix until smooth. Spread filling over cooled crust and refrigerate while you prepare fruit.

Arrange prepared fruit over filling.

For glaze, combine sugar and cornstarch in saucepan. Add juices and stir until smooth. Bring to boil over medium heat. Cook and stir until thickened. Cool, and then brush over fruit. Refrigerate pizza 1 hour before serving.

Serves 12-16

Tea Cakes

With timeless good taste, this recipe is based on one that was written over 100 years ago.

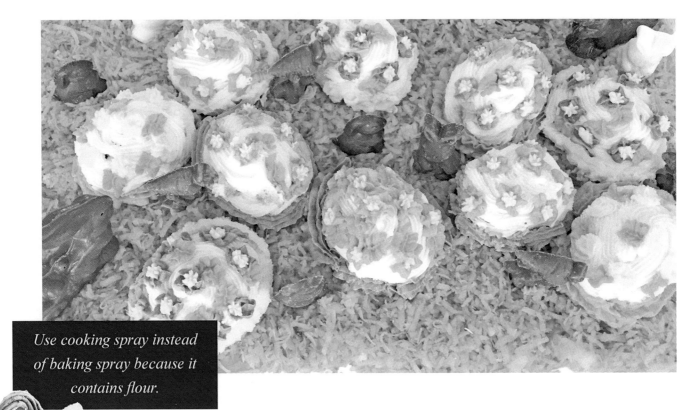

Use cooking spray instead of baking spray because it contains flour.

FROM THE PANTRY

1/2 cup butter, softened at room temperature

1/2 cup coconut oil

1-1/2 cups coconut sugar

2 eggs

2 teaspoons vanilla extract

1 cup coconut flour

1 cup brown rice flour

1/2 cup tapioca flour

1 teaspoon baking powder

1-1/2 teaspoons xanthan gum

1/4 salt

Sprinkles, optional

HOW TO CREATE

Cream butter, oil, and sugar.

Add eggs one at a time, mixing well after each addition. Add vanilla extract.

In separate bowl, combine flours and other dry ingredients, sifting them together. Coconut flour contains a lot of oil, so sifting is necessary to remove lumps.

Add flour mixture to creamed mixture and stir until combined. Rest dough for 15 minutes.

Preheat oven to 350°. Form a tablespoon of dough into ball, dip into small bowl of sprinkles, and flatten on a lightly oiled cookie sheet. Alternatively, you can scoop tablespoons of dough and flatten each scoop to form a cookie shape. Bake for 8-10 minutes.

Yields 3 dozen tea cakes

Lemon Filled Cupcakes

Little chocolate rabbits created by a dear friend made this yellow bouquet of cupcakes come alive! Spring is only a bite away with the creamy lemon filling in each center.

Olivia Lee loves her gluten-free cupcakes.

Cupcakes

FROM THE PANTRY

Two-layer gluten-free yellow cake mix

Additional ingredients on back of box

24 baking cups

HOW TO CREATE

Preheat oven to 350°.

Prepare cake mix according to directions. Line 24-cup muffin tin with baking cups. Fill cups and bake for 20-25 minutes. Transfer cupcakes to wire rack to cool completely.

Lemon Curd

FROM THE PANTRY

3 large egg yolks

1 teaspoon lemon zest

1/4 cup fresh lemon juice

7 tablespoons sugar

4 tablespoons cold butter

1 cup frozen whipped topping

HOW TO CREATE

Whisk together yolks, zest, lemon juice, and sugar in medium saucepan. Stirring constantly on medium heat, cook until mixture thickens, approximately 5-7 minutes. Remove from heat and add cold butter one slice at a time, stirring after each addition.

Transfer mixture to bowl, press plastic wrap onto surface, wrap bowl tightly, and refrigerate. Chill until firm, at least 1 hour. Combine lemon mixture with 1 cup frozen whipped topping.

To assemble cupcakes, cut 1-inch hole in middle of cupcake and place 1 tablespoon lemon curd mixture in hole. Top with your favorite butter cream frosting.

To make bouquet basket, choose container and round Styrofoam shape to fit inside container. Cover Styrofoam with green papier-mâché. Place 8-inch wooden skewers randomly in Styrofoam to hold cupcakes.

Yields 24 cupcakes

Pumpkin Chiffon Pie

Whoever authored the original version of this recipe is one of my invisible best friends. I love them, and I don't even know them! Just like turkey, this recipe is standard fare for both Thanksgiving and Christmas. The combination of each layer is a dream come true with every bite.

FROM THE PANTRY

1-3/4 cups gluten-free graham style crumbs

1/4 cup sugar

1/4 cup melted butter

8 ounces cream cheese, softened at room temperature

3/4 cup sugar

2 eggs

2 3.9-ounce boxes French vanilla instant pudding

3/4 cup milk

15-ounce can pumpkin

3 cups frozen whipped topping, divided

1/4 teaspoon cinnamon

1/4 cup chopped pecans

HOW TO CREATE

Preheat oven to 350°.

In medium bowl, combine first 3 ingredients and pat into lightly oiled 9x13 casserole dish to form crust.

With mixer, beat cream cheese and sugar until fluffy, 3-4 minutes. Reduce to low speed, add eggs, and mix well. Pour over crust and bake for 20-25 minutes. Place dish on wire rack and cool completely.

In large mixing bowl, mix pudding and milk, and then add pumpkin, 1 cup whipped topping, and cinnamon. Mix well. Pour over cooled cream cheese. Top with remaining whipped topping and sprinkle pecans on top.

Serves 12-15

Gingerbread

Every Christmas my family has a special guest: the gingerbread boy. We give him a special place where everyone can enjoy his company. Let me warn you, though. The first bite is always the hardest. Just where do you start? My recommendation is to start with a foot. Then he's sure not to run away! Whether baked in a 9x13 pan, a large gingerbread boy pan, or as individual cookies, this guest will surely be a holiday favorite.

Buckwheat flour is naturally gluten free. The origin of its name comes from its wheat-like consistency and usage.

FROM THE PANTRY

2-1/2 cups buckwheat flour (naturally gluten free)

2-1/2 cups sweet sorghum flour

1/2 cup tapioca starch

2 teaspoons xanthan gum

1 teaspoon baking soda

1 teaspoon salt

2 teaspoons ground ginger

2 teaspoons cinnamon

1 teaspoon nutmeg

1 teaspoon ground cloves

1 cup shortening

1 cup sugar

1-1/2 cups molasses

2 eggs, beaten

HOW TO CREATE

Preheat oven to 325°.

Whisk together first 10 ingredients.

Melt shortening in microwave. In mixing bowl, mix together melted shortening and sugar, beating for 3 minutes. Add molasses and continue beating; add eggs and mix well.

Add dry ingredients 1/2 cup at a time, mixing well after each addition. Let dough rest for 30 minutes.

Place dough in lightly oiled 9x13 pan and bake for 25-30 minutes or until toothpick inserted near center comes out clean. You may also half the dough and place in lightly oiled gingerbread boy shaped pans to make two large thick cookies. Bake these for 20-25 minutes. Or you may also make individual cookies and bake for 9-12 minutes.

Cool in pan for 5 minutes, and then remove to wire rack. Decorate with various candies and frosting.

Serves 20

Coconut Cashew Cookies

One of my favorite discoveries in gluten-free cooking has been coconut flour, sugar, and oil. These three products expanded creative horizons and gave way to new cooking adventures. Enjoy the coconut taste blended with cashews and chocolate in this thick, substantial mound of delight.

FROM THE PANTRY

1 cup coconut sugar

1 cup butter, softened at room temperature

2 eggs

1-1/2 teaspoons vanilla extract

1 cup coconut flour

1 cup oat flour

1/2 cup tapioca flour

1-1/2 teaspoons baking powder

1 teaspoon xanthan gum

1/4 teaspoon salt

1/4 teaspoon baking soda

11 ounces Hershey's Kisses

2 cups chopped cashews

1/2 cup coconut

HOW TO CREATE

Cream sugar and butter, and then add eggs and vanilla extract.

In separate bowl, combine dry ingredients and add to creamed mixture. Let dough rest for 15 minutes. Preheat oven to 350°. Chop Kisses into small pieces.

Toast cashews and coconut together in 300° oven until lightly browned. Stir nut mixture and Kisses into cookie dough.

Cover baking sheet with parchment paper. By tablespoons, form dough into balls and place on baking sheet. Slightly flatten each ball of dough. Bake for 9 minutes. Cool for 1 minute on baking sheet, and then transfer to wire rack.

Yields 2 dozen cookies